J 920 PARKER
Parker, Steve. 200374 c.3
The Wright brothers and aviation
$ 13.37   19903887
Flint River Regional Library 1995

W9-BAA-791

Governor Zell Miller's
Reading Initiative

NoLex 113

Peachtree City Library
201 Willowbend Rd.
Peachtree City, GA 30269-1623

GAYLORD FG

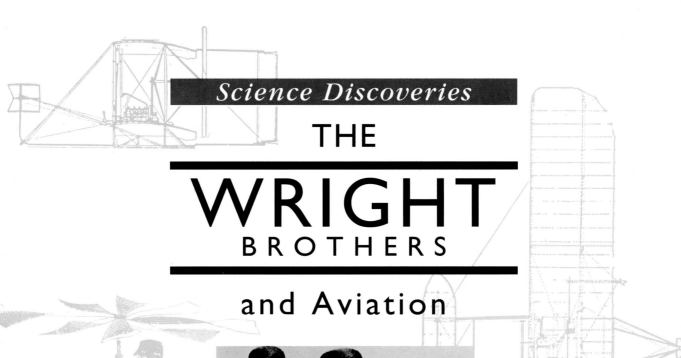

Science Discoveries

THE
WRIGHT
BROTHERS
and Aviation

Steve Parker

Chelsea House Publishers
New York • Philadelphia

FLINT RIVER REGIONAL LIBRARY

This edition © Chelsea House Publishers 1995

First published in Great Britain in 1994 by
Belitha Press Limited, 31 Newington Green,
London N16 9PU

Copyright © Belitha Press Ltd 1994

Text © Steve Parker 1994

Illustrations/photographs © in this format by
Belitha Press Limited 1994

All rights reserved.

1 3 5 7 9 8 6 4 2

ISBN 0-7910-3013-X

Acknowledgments

Photographic credits:
Bridgeman Art Library 10 top Bibliothèque de
l'Institute, Paris.
Mary Evans Picture Library 11 bottom, 19 top, 24 left,
25 top.
Hulton Deutsch Collection 22 top left, 23 bottom.
Image Select 5 bottom left and 7 top Nick Birch, 8
top,17 bottom left Smithsonian Institution, 21 top,
23 inset, 26 top.
Mansell Collection 7 bottom, 8 bottom, 9.
Oxford Scientific Films 13 bottom Godfrey Merlen.
Science Photo Library 26 bottom left, 27 top right
NASA, 27 bottom Carlos Goldin.
TRH Pictures titlepage, 24 right and 29 NASM,11
top,15 bottom, 22 top right, 26 bottom right, 27 top
left.
Wright State University 4, 5 top and center right, 6
both,14 top,16 bottom, 17 bottom right,18 bottom
left, 20 top, 21 bottom, 25 background and bottom.

Cover images provided by Image Select

Illustrations by Tony Smith
Diagrams by Peter Bull

Editor: Phil Roxbee Cox
Design: Cooper Wilson Limited
Picture research: Juliet Duff

Library of Congress Cataloging-in-Publication Data

Parker, Steve.
 The Wright brothers and aviation / Steve Parker
  p. cm. (Science Discoveries)
 Includes index.
 ISBN 0-7910-3013-X
 1. Wright, Orville. 1871-1948--Juvenile literature.
 2. Wright, Wilbur. 1867-1912--Juvenile literature.
 3. Aeronautics--United States--Biography--Juvenile
 literature. [1. Wright, Orville, 1871-1948. 2. Wright,
 Wilbur, 1867-1912. 3. Aeronautics--Biography.]
 I. Title. II. Series: Parker, Steve. Science discoveries.
 TL540.W7P32 1995
 629. 13'0092'2--dc20
 [B]   94-25254
                                            CIP
                                             AC

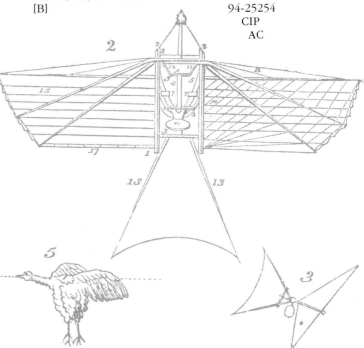

Contents

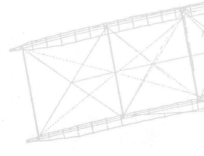

Introduction

At this moment, there are thousands of aircraft in the skies around the world. They are different shapes and sizes, according to their jobs. Tourists fly in comfortable airliners on exotic holidays. Businesspeople dash to meetings in executive jets. Cargo planes transport freight and air mail. Spotter planes give traffic reports, and survey planes take aerial photographs. Helicopters look for the lost or stranded, while air-ambulances rush the injured to hospitals. Military aircraft patrol trouble spots, ready for action, while high in the sky, spy planes keep track of enemies – and friends.

The age of the airplane and controlled, **powered flight** is less than a hundred years old. It began in 1903, on the cold and windswept coast near Kitty Hawk, North Carolina. Two brothers from Dayton, Ohio, named Wilbur and Orville Wright, had designed and built their own wood-and-fabric craft, the *Flyer.* They took turns piloting it on its first flights, spluttering unsteadily only a few yards above the sands.

Wilbur (left) and Orville Wright were both born on August 19, but four years apart.

Chapter One
The Early Years

From early childhood, Wilbur and Orville Wright were more like twins than brothers. They shared interests and ambitions. Wilbur once said that they "played together, worked together and, in fact, thought together."

Wilbur was born on a farm near Milville, Indiana, on August 19, 1867. The family moved to Dayton, Ohio, where Orville was born on August 19, 1871, at 7 Hawthorn Street. They had two older brothers, Reuchlin and Lorin, and a younger sister, Katharine.

Their father, Milton Wright, became a bishop of the United Brethren Church. He was sometimes away from home for long periods. He taught his sons that with hard work and a will to succeed, they could achieve almost anything. During their schooldays Orville and Wilbur were always messing about with machines and playing with kites.

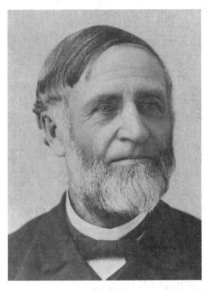

Susan Koerner Wright, mother of Wilbur and Orville, was a shy woman who was skilled with her hands. She helped and encouraged her sons with their interest in mechanical things. Their father, Milton Wright, became a bishop in Iowa.

The Wrights' family home in Hawthorn Street, Dayton, Ohio.

When Katharine went to college in Ohio, a housekeeper looked after Wilbur, Orville, and their father. Katharine graduated in 1898 and returned to Dayton as a teacher.

The "bat"

In 1878, Milton Wright was appointed a bishop and the family moved to Cedar Rapids, Iowa. One day he brought home a toy for his two youngest sons. It was a helicopter made of wood and paper, with **propellers** powered by a rubber band. Wilbur and Orville called it the "bat". They played with it endlessly. When it broke, they mended it. When it fell to pieces, they built new versions. But when they tried a much bigger design, it did not fly well. They could not understand why. The "bat began their interest in flying machines.

A Sad Loss

In 1889, Susan Wright died of consumption (tuberculosis). Wilbur had looked after his mother during her long illness. He had been ill, too, after a sports injury while playing hockey at school in 1885. His face was smashed by an opponent's stick, and he needed surgery and false teeth. Then he developed digestive and heart trouble.

The two older brothers, Reuchlin and Lorin, left home. For a time, Katharine Wright took over her mother's role in the family.

A Start in Printing

Bishop Wright was very involved in editing and publishing church newspapers. As teenagers, the brothers also became interested in newspapers and printing. Wilbur helped to write and edit his father's paper. He invented a machine to fold the papers before they were mailed.

During holidays, Orville helped at a local printing works. He also made his own presses, from leftover parts and bits of junk. Then he left school early to work in printing, hiring his friend Ed Sines to be his assistant.

An early edition of the Wright brothers' weekly local paper, the West Side News

In March 1890, Orville started a local weekly newspaper, the *West Side News*. He was the publisher, and Wilbur joined as editor. The paper ran for a year. However, an attempt to change it to a daily paper, *The Evening Item*, failed.

From Papers to Bicycles

Next, the brothers and Ed Sines set up as Wright and Wright, Job Printers. They worked hard, producing posters, ads, leaflets, and cards, and built up the business.

Soon bicycles took over from printing. Ed Sines was put in charge of the printing business. Wilbur and Orville set up The Wright Cycle Company. They opened a shop at 1127 West Third Street, Dayton, then started more shops. They sold bicycles, repaired and rented them, and began to design and make their own models. In future years, the money from the cycle business would allow the Wrights to spend many months on their flying machines.

The Wright Brothers' bicycle shop at 1127 West Third Street, Dayton, as it appears today in the Wright State University Museum.

In the 1890s, a bicycle craze was sweeping the land. The new "safety bicycle" had air-filled tires, wheels of equal size, and pedals that worked a chain.

The French, brothers Joseph and Etienne Montgolfier, designed and built the first hot-air balloons to carry people.

All Things Mechanical

The Wrights constantly taught themselves more skills with machines and mechanics. They worked with metals and woods and used tools such as drills and lathes. They even made a small **combustion engine** to power their workshop machinery.

During the late 1890s, the Wright brothers' interests moved on again. Gliding was in the news. It was said that one day a person would achieve real powered flight. Whoever did this would become famous and wealthy. Remembering the kites and "bat" toy of their childhood, the Wrights decided that they wanted to build a flying machine.

Pilâtre de Rozier and the Marquis d'Arlandes aboard the Montgolfier balloon in 1783.

Lighter than Air

Long before the Wright brothers, people had taken to the air in flying machines. But most of these were lighter-than-air balloons and **airships** or gliders (see page 10).

1783 First aloft was French scientist François Pilâtre de Rozier. He rose in a hot-air balloon made by two brothers, Joseph and Etienne Montgolfier. The balloon was tied to the ground by a rope. A few weeks later, de Rozier and the Marquis d'Arlandes made the first free balloon flight, 5 miles over Paris, in another of the Montgolfier brothers' balloons.

1852 The first airship flight was by Frenchman Henry Giffard. Coal gas filled the cigar-shaped balloon, and a steam engine turned the propeller.

1900 The golden age of airships began in 1900 with the first of the famous zeppelins. But airships were dangerous — the light **hydrogen** gas in them would catch fire, and their fragile frames were easily torn in storms.

1937 The giant airship *Hindenberg* crashed in flames, killing 36 people, and the airship era finally ended.

Chapter Two
The Skills of Gliding

How could Wilbur and Orville make a true flying machine? Several full-time scientist-engineers had tried and failed. The Wrights had no detailed training in science or **engineering**.

But they did have self-taught skills in design and machinery. They approached the challenge with careful stage-by-stage planning, common sense and quiet determination. (Most of the time, Wilbur took the lead in planning.) They also had a number of lucky breaks along the way.

Pioneer in the Air

The Wrights were greatly inspired by Otto Lilienthal (see panel right), who had been inspired, in turn, by the Englishman George Cayley.

Cayley invented artificial limbs, caterpillar tracks for vehicles, and other devices. He was also interested in flight. In 1804, he built and flew the first successful model **glider**. In 1849, at age 76, he built a glider with three sets of wings and a boat-hull body. Towed on a rope like a kite, it swooped a short distance, carrying a 10-year-old boy.

A Gliding Tragedy

On August 9, 1896, there was a tragic accident in Germany. Engineer Otto Lilienthal, who had been building and flying gliders for several years, was piloting a glider that was suddenly caught by a side wind. The craft crashed to the ground. Lilienthal broke his back and died the next day.

Lilienthal was the leading glider expert of the time. He had designed and built at least 16 different gliders, made of wood and wire frames covered by muslin. He carried out about 2,000 flights, the longest lasting 15 seconds.

Otto Lilienthal with one of his flying contraptions. His flights, and the tragedy of his death, inspired Wilbur and Orville to learn everything they could about gliding and flying.

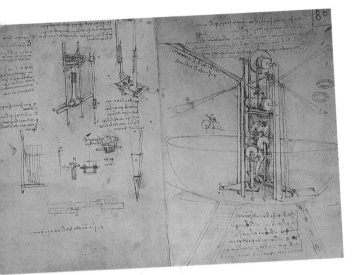

Leonardo da Vinci (1452-1519) was a scientist and engineer as well as a great sculptor and painter. This da Vinci sketch is his idea for a flying machine.

Attempts at Powered Flight

The Wrights were far from the first to build a powered flying machine. The difference was that the others were too heavy to stay in the air for long.

1842 William Henson and John Stringfield designed an elegant *Aerial Steam Carriage*. Though never built, its design influenced many later pioneers.

1857 Frenchman Félix du Temple built a model plane powered by a clockwork motor, later changed to a tiny steam engine. These models were the first aircraft to achieve powered, sustained flight, but they could not carry people.

1874 Du Temple's full-sized, steam-driven machine stayed in the air for a few yards after rushing down its takeoff ramp but could not make a sustained flight.

1884 Russian Alexander Mozhaiski's craft remained in the air for a few seconds, also after a takeoff from a ramp.

1890 Clément Ader of France tested his steam-driven, bat-winged *Eole* machine. It flew for about 50 yards, but stayed less than a yard above the ground, and its flight could not be controlled.

1894 Hiram Maxim, inventor of the machine gun, made a short hop in his steam-powered, four-winged machine.

Bird-men Through the Ages

Through the ages, many people had ideas about flying like the birds.

Ancient Greece Legend tells how Daedelus and his son, Icarus, made arm-wings of wax and bird feathers, to escape from King Minos of Crete. Icarus flew too near the Sun, the wax melted, and he fell into the sea.

Eleventh century At Wiltshire Abbey, England, a monk named Eilmer tried to glide from the tower. His arm and leg wings were covered with bird feathers. He crashed and broke both legs.

Early 1500s Italian artist and scientist Leonardo da Vinci sketched designs for several flying machines. Some had rotating screw-like wings, others flapping ones powered by the body's muscles.

1685 Italian scientist Giovanni Borelli showed that human muscles were not big or strong enough to keep the body's weight in the air, using flapping wings.

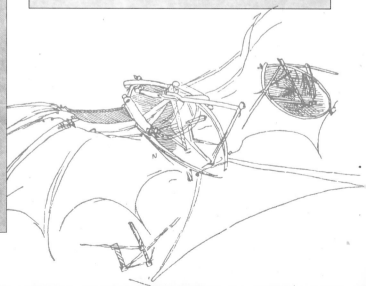

Three Problems

Sir George Cayley devised the basic airplane shape as we still know it – long, fixed wings, a central **fuselage**, a tail for controlling direction, and a small, powerful, lightweight engine. But there were no lightweight engines in his day.

Some pioneers of powered flight worked with small models of aircraft, driven by miniature engines. If these were successful, they would build larger versions. But the Wrights decided on the "powered glider" approach. They would develop a full-sized gliding machine, practice flying and controlling it, and then add an engine.

First, they would have to solve three main problems. These were the problems of designing the best wings to lift the craft, finding a means of controlling it in the air, and building a power plant to propel it. With this in mind, the Wrights took up birdwatching.

Octave Chanute (1832 - 1910)

Octave Chanute

Another gliding pioneer, who read about the work of Cayley and others, was Octave Chanute. He was an American engineer famous for large projects such as building a long bridge over the Missouri River.

Chanute had visited Lilienthal in Germany to discuss gliding and flying. From 1896 to 1898, Chanute and his team built and flew several Lilienthal-type hang gliders. They made hundreds of flights in the steady, strong breezes that blew over the sand dunes of Lake Michigan's southern shore.

Lilienthal, Chanute, and others published their experiments and results in scientific magazines and books. Chanute became the leading figure in America for information and reports on the science of flight. The Wrights asked him for advice, and they became friends, writing regular letters to each other.

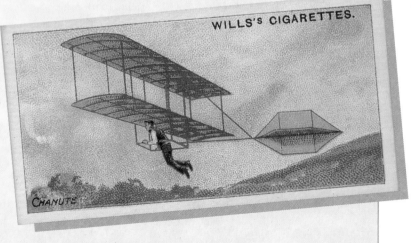

WILLS'S CIGARETTES.

CHANUTE

Chapter Three
The Windswept Sands

In 1899, Wilbur Wright wrote to the famous Smithsonian Institution in Washington, D.C. He asked for information on flying machines: "I wish to avail myself of all that is already known." The Institution sent him books and pamphlets by Octave Chanute (see page 11), Samuel Langley and other pioneers and experimenters.

Lifting Wings

One major decision for the Wrights was wing shape. This may seem strange to us today, when we are familiar with many different types of wings, from the swept-back wings of a jet fighter to the long thin wings of a glider. But the Wrights had no aircraft to copy. There was only a handful of experimental winged craft in the whole world.

Lilienthal, Chanute, and others had shown that a wing should be curved on its top surface. This shape is called the **airfoil** section. As the wing moves forwards, it creates an upward force called **lift** (see panel).

Wings and Airfoils

An aircraft wing is curved more on top than the underneath. In flight, the effect of this shape is to produce lower **air pressure** on the upper surface of the wing than on the lower, in such a way that a lifting force is produced by the "suction" on the upper surface. The Wrights also experimented with many other wing shapes, proportions and dimensions, as shown in the picture below.

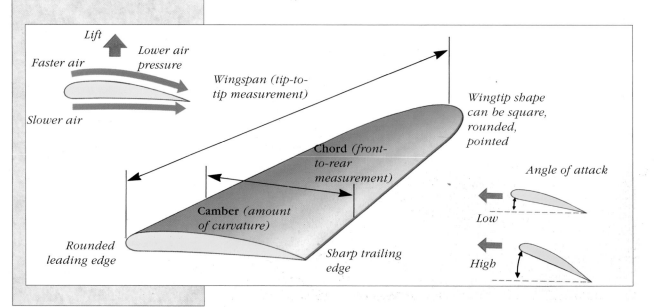

Lift

Faster air

Lower air pressure

Slower air

Wingspan (tip-to-tip measurement)

Wingtip shape can be square, rounded, pointed

Chord (front-to-rear measurement)

Angle of attack

Camber (amount of curvature)

Low

Rounded leading edge

Sharp trailing edge

High

Control in the Air

In Lilienthal's hang gliders, the pilot's body hung below the craft. He controlled the glider by shifting his body weight forwards and back, and from side to side. A bigger, heavier powered craft would need more than shifting body weight to control it.

To turn a flying machine left or right, the Wrights borrowed an idea from boats – the vertical **rudder**. Swing it to the left, and the air rushing past would push it to the right, making the craft turn left. This was used on their 1902 glider.

To go up or down, they used a "horizontal rudder" called an **elevator**. Swing it, and the air rushing past would push on it, making the craft go up or down. On Wright planes, the elevators were at the front; on most aircraft today, they are at the rear.

Warping Wings

But what about tilting or **banking** a plane from side to side, known as rolling? Wilbur and Orville spent hours watching buzzards and other birds soaring over the hills near their home. The birds seemed to twist their wings, especially at the tips. But how could a stiff airplane wing do this?

Three Ways to Go

A car on the ground has only one directional control – the steering wheel to turn left or right. A plane has three directional controls, as shown below:

Ailerons *or wing-warp* control **roll** *(tilt or bank)*

Rudder controls **yaw** *(left or right)*

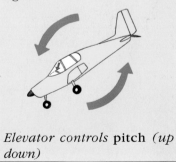

Elevator controls **pitch** *(up down)*

The Wright brothers noted how birds twisted or warped their wings to turn and manouvre in the air.

This hut, in the Wright brothers' camp at Kitty Hawk, doubled as a kitchen and aircraft workshop.

The Wrights did not want others stealing their ideas and aircraft designs. Kitty Hawk was an ideal place to work in secret.

Wilbur solved this puzzle while fiddling with a long, thin cardboard box in their bicycle shop. He suddenly saw how two wings, one above the other, could twist along their length, to control roll in the air. If the wing ends were flexible, they could be twisted or "warped" by a system of cables and pulleys. The wingtip that twisted up would be pushed down by the air rushing past, and the craft would roll to that side. (Aircraft today use hinged surfaces called ailerons to do the same job.)

Off to the Seaside

The Wrights quickly could now build their first aircraft. It was a double-winged glider with control lines to twist the wings. They tested it on a nearby hill, where they had flown kites as boys. It worked perfectly.

The next job was to build a larger glider, big enough to carry a pilot, and to find a place with regular winds to test it. They chose Kitty Hawk, a fishing village on the Outer Banks, on the east coast of North Carolina.

Kitty Hawk was remote and isolated, surrounded by miles of empty, windswept sand dunes. It was ideal, with strong winds that averaged 9 miles per hour. The sand was soft for landings, with no trees or rocks.

The 1900 Glider

In September 1900, the brothers traveled by train, ferry, and hired boat to Kitty Hawk. They lived in a tent on the windy dunes, where sand blew everywhere. They had brought their first large glider. It was a double-decker or **biplane** design, with a **wingspan** of 5.7 yards, a wooden frame, and woven cotton covering. The pilot lay on the lower wing. He operated the front elevator with his hands and the wing-warp by a pivoted bar at his feet.

After three weeks of unmanned tests, they took the glider along the shore, with help from the local postmaster, Bill Tate. Their launch site was a group of three huge sand dunes called Kill Devil Hills. Wilbur made the first test glides into the strong winds. The best covered over 100 yards in about 20 seconds. But the winds died down, and the brothers returned to Dayton.

Before trying to put a person on board a glider, the Wrights tested various glider designs, flying them like kites.

The 1900 glider, pictured below at Kitty Hawk, was first flown by Wilbur.

The 1901 Glider

During the winter, the Wrights built a bigger glider. Its wingspan was 7.4 yards, and its chord 2.2 yards. The wing-warp system was now worked by a hip cradle, a "seat" in which the pilot lay. By shifting his hips to the side, he worked cables and pulleys that twisted the wing tips.

In July 1901, the Wrights were back at Kitty Hawk. They built a wooden shed for the new glider near Big Hill, the largest of Kill Devil Hills. Once again they lived in a tent, plagued by wind, sand, and mosquitoes. Octave Chanute visited them, showed polite interest, and soon left.

Wilbur at the controls of the bigger 1901 glider, which was less successful than the brothers had hoped.

The 1901 glider is subjected to further tests while being flown like a kite.

Several Setbacks

The new glider was only partly successful. As the glider banked, it tended to go out of control, into a steep spin.

The Wrights made on-the-spot adjustments and managed a few reasonable glides. But Wilbur crash-landed, damaging the glider and his face. They repaired the glider and tested it further as a kite, but the rains came and dampened their hopes. At the end of August they packed up and went home to Dayton. Wilbur said: "We considered our experiments a failure. I made the prediction that man would sometime fly, but that it would not be in our lifetime."

Chapter Four
The First Flight

The Wright brothers thought about the problems of their 1901 glider. They decided they should not have used the information of Lilienthal and others, about wing areas and lifting forces. Wilbur wrote: "We cast it all aside, and decided to rely entirely on our own investigations."

So Wilbur and Orville decided to experiment with model wings, testing different shapes, airfoils, wingtips and other features. They built a simple wind tunnel, from wooden orange boxes, that was 2 yards long. It had a large fan at one end, driven by the workshop's gas-powered engine, and a viewing window in the top.

During October and November 1901, the Wrights made over 150 model wings from thin sheet metal. They devised an ingenious system of pivoted, swinging arms to compare the lift produced by each wing and the **resistance** or **drag** caused by the air rushing over them.

Visits from Family and Friends

Older brother Lorin used to visit Wilbur and Orville at Kitty Hawk. So did Octave Chanute and his assistants. One of these was George Spratt, who came because of his interest in flying and because he had medical training – in case of an accident. Spratt became a close and valued friend of the Wrights. Dan Tate, a member of a local family, also helped regularly with glider and plane launches.

The Wright brothers always maintained their boyhood enthusiasm for kites. The influences of birds is obvious in this particular design.

This wind tunnel is similar to the one the Wrights used to test the effect of air movement on different shaped wings.

The Aerodrome's Splash-landing

Eminent scientist Professor Samuel Langley, secretary of the famous Smithsonian Institution, also worked on powered flight. He tested models first. On October 7, 1903, his full-sized, four-winged craft *Great Aerodrome* was ready. It was launched by a catapult along special rails on the roof of a houseboat in the Potomac River, Washington D.C. But the *Great Aerodrome* flopped straight into the water.

On December 8, there was a second attempt – and another immediate splash-landing. Some of the newspapers had great fun, saying that Langley should design not flying machines but submarines!

The 1902 Glider

Using their newfound knowledge, the Wright brothers designed their 1902 glider, the biggest yet. Its wings were longer but less broad, with a wingspan of 10.8 yards and chord of 1.6 yards. A hip cradle worked the wing-warp system. There was an elevator at the front and, for the first time, a tail – two upright, fixed fins. The design worked well, and the Wrights made hundreds of glides. There was only one crash-landing, but the Wrights' luck, which saved them so many times, did not fail. The machine ended up as "cloth and sticks in a heap," yet pilot Orville was unhurt.

Total Control

One problem was that now and again, the glider banked too steeply and spun around and down like a corkscrew. Orville suggested making the tail fins moveable, like a ship's rudder. Wilbur added that the rudder could be worked by wires linked to the wing-warp system. The changes were made, and the results were excellent. They now had control in the air. The next step was propeller power.

Another pioneer in the race for the first true flight was Samuel Langley (see left panel). This newspaper article tells of his disastrous efforts in 1903.

Building the Flyer

Hardly anyone had tested different propeller designs in a scientific way. The Wrights were the first people to understand that a propeller should be like a wing that turns round and round. It creates lift in a forward direction and "sucks" itself along, as well as pushing air backwards.

On September 25, 1903 the brothers were back on the windy sands near Kitty Hawk, assembling their powered flying machine, the *Flyer*.

Last-minute Hitch

When Wilbur and Orville heard that Samuel Langley was planning a flight for December 8 (see left panel), they hurriedly fixed a new engine and propellers to the *Flyer*. On December 14, the toss of a coin decided that Wilbur would be the first pilot. His takeoff was too steep, and the craft crashed back down after only 3.5 seconds.

At the turn of the century, there were many newfangled inventions, including steam-powered carriages and gas-powered cars.

The Engine

The practical internal combustion engine had been around for about 20 years. It powered the new automobiles appearing around the countryside, as well as boats and workshop machines. The brothers calculated they needed an engine that weighed less than 200 pounds and produced 8 horsepower (6,000 watts). But no manufacturer made such a light, powerful engine. So the Wrights designed and built their own in their bicycle workshop, with their mechanic Charles Taylor. It weighed 180 pounds and produced over 12 horsepower.

The 1903 Flyer *is held above the windswept sands of Kitty Hawk ready for takeoff.*

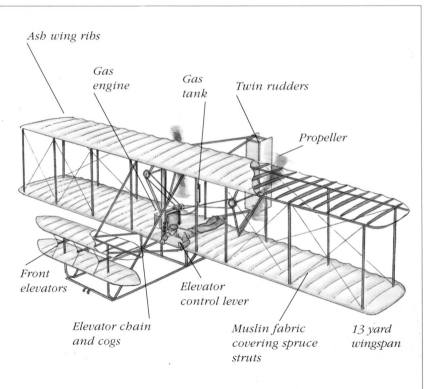

One of the most famous photographs in science, showing Orville's first flight. Wilbur flew the furthest that day – a distance of 286 yards in 59 seconds.

History Is Made

Three days later, on Thursday, December 17, the propellers whirred and the motor spluttered into life again. It was 10:35 AM. Orville released the brake cable and the *Flyer* trundled forward on its launch rail, straight into the 47–mph wind.

Wilbur and the few onlookers cheered as Orville worked the controls. The *Flyer* rose into the air, to the agreed height of 3 to 5 yards. It lurched up and down. But it was flying! After 12 seconds, the craft landed 40 yards from its takeoff point. It had taken off from level ground and flown in a controlled, sustained way under its own power – the first true flight. Three more flights followed that morning.

The *Flyer*'s Features

For takeoff, the *Flyer* rested on a small wheeled trolley known as the truck. This ran along a metal-covered launch rail made from four 5-yard lengths of wood. A person ran along steadying the wingtip, until the pilot gained control. Then the *Flyer* rose, leaving the trolley behind. Its propeller blades rotated in opposite directions to keep the plane in balance. The *Flyer* landed on its skids on the sand.

The Flyer*'s pitch was controlled by its front elevators. Banking was controlled by the pilot moving from side to side.*

Ash wing ribs

Gas engine

Gas tank

Twin rudders

Propeller

Front elevators

Elevator control lever

Elevator chain and cogs

Muslin fabric covering spruce struts

13 yard wingspan

Chapter Five
Toward a Practical Plane

The Wrights planned more flights in the afternoon, but at their finest hour, their luck failed. As they stood talking, the wind got under the *Flyer*'s wings and rolled it along the sand. The flying machine was badly damaged. The Wrights packed and went home.

There was some interest in the news of the first true flight. But many people thought it was a trick, especially after the *Aerodrome* disaster. The newspapers and authorities demanded another flight, in public. The Wrights refused. If people saw the *Flyer*, they might try to copy it.

Home from Home

Wilbur and Orville knew their first flights were only short and straight. They wanted to improve the *Flyer* so that it could rise, descend, and turn under good control, for long periods. In 1904, at Huffman's Pasture, near Dayton, they built a workshed and a second *Flyer*, a stronger and more powerful machine. Here the brothers devised a new system to give the plane extra speed on a launch rail.

These markers at Kitty Hawk indicate the position and distances covered by the Flyer *in its early flights.*

"That Ridiculous Flying Machine"

Even two years after the first flight, most people thought that flying machines had no future. The *Interurban* electric trolley line ran near Huffman's Pasture, and the Wrights tried to avoid flying planes when the trolley-cars passed every half-hour. But several passengers saw them. One said: "They seemed like well-meaning decent young men. Yet there they were, neglecting their business to waste their time, day after day, on that ridiculous flying machine."

A 1904 Flyer *takes off over Simms Station at Huffman's Pasture for one of many test flights.*

Other Americans interested in powered flight included Glenn Curtiss. His first successful flight was not until 1908.

Planes for Sale

By the end of 1905, the Wright brothers knew that they had a truly practical plane. For the next two years, they tried to sell it without showing it in public. They knew that rivals were waiting to steal their ideas and designs.

Wilbur then approached the U.S. War Department, Britain, and then other governments. He said that he needed a signed contract, promising money if the *Flyer* performed as agreed. He also wanted to have control over the airplane's manufacturing and servicing business. But he made little progress.

Better and Better

In 1905 the Wrights designed and built their third *Flyer*. One important change was to the control system. Instead of linking the rudder to the wing-warp system, it had its own lever. The pilot had three controls – the hip cradle for the wing-warp (roll), a hand lever for the elevator (pitch), and another hand lever for the rudder (yaw).

In this *Flyer* the Wrights set new records. Wilbur flew around the Huffman's Pasture field 39 times, covering 25 miles in 29 minutes.

Progress in Europe

The Wrights continued to develop their fourth plane, the *Wright Type A Flyer*. In this version the pilot sat upright in a chair. Two hand levers worked the elevator, rudder, and wing-warping. And there would be a passenger.

In 1906, in France, a rich Brazilian inventor, Alberto Santos-Dumont, became the third person to fly successfully in a powered machine heavier than air. His unsteady craft, the *14-Bis,* looked like several box-kites joined together, with the rudder and elevators at the front. His best flight was 242 yards in 21 seconds.

"Fliers or Liars?"

The Wrights knew that other aviators might eventually catch up. They agreed to demonstration flights for the U.S. Army. On May 14, 1908, practicing back at historic Kill Devil Hills, they made another first – a two-person flight, with Dayton mechanic Charlie Furnas as passenger.

In May 1908, Wilbur sailed for France with a *Flyer* in crates. It was damaged on the journey and took several weeks to repair. The French newspapers became impatient. They found it hard to believe that the Wrights could turn, bank, swoop, and dive an airplane at will. Headlines such as "Fliers or Liars?" appeared, and the Wrights became known as "Les Bluffeurs."

Finally, on August 8, Wilbur took up his *Wright Type A* at a racetrack near Le Mans, France. Compared to the unsteady French flights, his smooth banks and turns created a sensation.

World Fame

Wilbur made over 100 flights in France in late 1908 and early 1909. Spectators screamed and swooned, and all the newspapers went wild. French aviator René Gasnier said: "We are but children compared to the Wrights." Louis Blériot (see page 25) was "speechless." The brothers had won world fame at last.

(Far left) The Wrights' success captured the imagination of the press in Europe.

A Wright Type A Flyer *cruises past one of the world's most famous landmarks, the Eiffel Tower in Paris.*

Chapter Six

The Later Years

While Wilbur stayed in France, Orville returned to Dayton to work on a new *Flyer* for the Army Signal Corps. Other American aviators were also working hard, and during 1908 Glenn Curtiss and Douglas McCurdy flew planes. In September 1908, Orville made demonstration flights for the army at Fort Myer, Virginia. Thousands of people watched in amazement as he stayed aloft for over an hour, circling, banking, and diving.

Seeing Is Believing

In 1909, Wilbur made more flights in France, then in Italy. Crowds still flocked to see him and watched in amazement. There was no television and people were still wary about "the miracle of flight." They would only believe it after seeing it with their own eyes.

The First Fatality

On September 17, 1908, Orville was flying with passenger Lieutenant Thomas Selfridge. One of the *Flyer*'s propellers split and hit a bracing wire. The plane crashed down from a height of 30 yards. Selfridge died a few hours later, the first fatality of a powered-plane crash. Orville was in the hospital for seven weeks with severe injuries.

A dramatic illustration of the accident which killed Thomas Selfridge and badly injured Orville Wright.

A Wright brothers' plane weighed so little that it could easily be towed to a flying field by an ordinary motorcar of the period.

Two months after the Wrights' celebrated return home, the Frenchman Louis Blériot (1872-1936) became the first man to fly across the English Channel, in a plane of his own design.

Flying in a Skirt

At Camp d'Auvours in France, Mrs. Hart Berg became the first woman to fly, as Wilbur's passenger. To keep her long skirt from flapping in the breeze, it was tied with a cord just above her ankles. She hobbled away from the plane before the cord was removed – and created the fashionable 1909 hobble skirt.

Triumphant Homecoming

The Wrights returned home via Paris, London, New York, and Washington, D.C. They arrived in Dayton on 13 May 1909, and were hailed as all-conquering heroes. In late July, Orville finished his flights for the U.S. Army, watched by President Howard Taft. The airplane more than met its promise, and the army paid. With all the contracts and manufacturing agreements, the Wrights were rich for life.

Flying Comes of Age

The Wrights continued to make progress. Their *Vin Fiz* made the first coast-to-coast trip across the U.S.A, taking 70 separate flights, or "hops," between September and December 1911.

In 1912, Wilbur fell ill with typhoid fever, and died on May 30. The world mourned, and all activity in Dayton stopped during the funeral.

Two years later, Orville, his father, and his sister moved into Hawthorn Hill, a large mansion in Dayton. In 1918 he gave up flying. He died on January 30, 1948 from a heart attack, having seen aircraft play an important role in World War II.

Enthusiastic crowds gather in Dayton, Ohio, to greet Orville and Wilbur on their return.

The Lockheed SR-71A Blackbird, *the world's fastest airplane, looks very different from the Wrights' first* Flyer. *The* Blackbird *is powered by jet engines. One of the first successfully flown jet planes was the Gloster Whittle E28/39 (bottom right).*

Chapter Seven

After The Wrights

In the 1920s, planes began to change daily life. They gradually became faster, more powerful, and more efficient. As with most types of technology, great progress was made during World War I, as each side tried to build better aircraft – first for spotting enemy positions, then for aerial **dogfights** and later for bombing raids.

The first air mail services started in 1918. The next year, John Alcock and Arthur Whitten Brown made the first nonstop Atlantic crossing in a converted Vickers Vimy bomber.

Regular passenger flights began in earnest in the 1920s. In 1924 two Douglas seaplanes flew around the world, in 57 "hops." In 1927 Charles Lindbergh made the first solo crossing of the Atlantic in his Ryan monoplane, *Spirit of St Louis.*

The jet engine was invented by the Englishman Sir Frank Whittle (below). This single invention changed the course of aviation history. Today, the world's biggest and fastest planes are all jet powered.

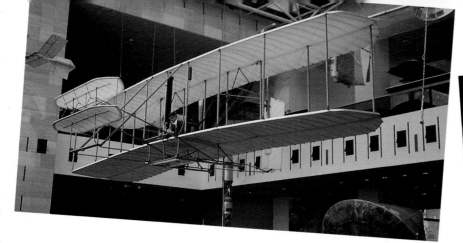

Everyday Flight

All these planes had internal combustion engines and propellers, like the Wrights' *Flyer*. During World War II, the first jets appeared, accelerating aircraft to new speed records. The Comet 4 and Boeing 707 jetlinerswere soon used to transport passengers at undreamed-of speeds.

Today millions of people fly in jet planes, on business trips and holidays. The world's largest jet, the Boeing 747 *Jumbo*, has a wingspan almost twice as long as the first flight made by the *Flyer*.

The original Flyer *now hangs in the National Air and Space Museum (top left). Mankind has now conquered space as well as the skies. In 1969, Neil Armstrong and Buzz Aldrin became the first people to walk on the Moon (above).*

Flights into the record books

In 1957, the age of space flight began, with the launch of the USSR's *Sputnik 1* satellite. On July 20, 1979, *Apollo 11* became the first craft to fly humans to the Moon. Neil Armstrong had a piece of cloth covering from the original *Flyer* with him when he stepped onto the Moon's surface.

Records continue to be set. In 1986, Dick Rutan and Jeana Jaeger flew nonstop around the world, taking nine days. Their craft, *Voyager,* is preserved in the National Air and Space Museum, in a position of honor near the plane that started it all – the Wrights' 1903 *Flyer.*

Today's ultralight aircraft are probably the nearest things to the Wrights' planes in the sky.

The World in The Wrights' Time

	1850-1875	1876-1900
Science	**1852** Henry Giffard builds the first powered lighter-than-air craft	**1876** Alexander Graham Bell patents his invention, the telephone
	1865 Joseph Lister begins the use of germ-killing antiseptics during surgical operations	**1883** Robert Koch identifies a tiny germ, the cholera bacterium, that causes the disease cholera, and shows how it can be spread in food and water
	1867 Wilbur Wright is born	
	1871 Orville Wright is born	
.Exploration	**1864** Samuel Baker travels up the Nile, confirming it flowed through Lake Albert Nyaza	**1871** Journalist Henry Stanley finds African explorer and medical missionary David Livingstone in Ujiji. Livingstone had lost contact with the outside world, and Stanley asks: "Dr Livingstone, I presume?"
	1867 American colonists move into Alaska as the US buys the region from Russia for $7.2 million	
		1897 The Yukon gold rush starts
Politics	**1852** President Louis Napoleon of France makes himself Emperor Napoleon III, beginning the French Second Empire	**1870-71** Germany becomes one united nation under Otto von Bismarck, who becomes prince and chancellor
	1861-65 American Civil War	**1885-94** Karl Marx publishes the second and third parts of *Das Kapital*
	1863 The Ionian Islands are given by Britain to Greece	
Art	**1860** Charles Dickens publishes *Great Expectations*	**1880** Gilbert and Sullivan finish their light opera *The Pirates of Penzance*
	1861 Architect Charles Garnier wins a competition with his ornate, expensive design for the Paris Opera House (opened in 1875)	**1882** Paul Cézanne paints his *Self-Portrait*

1903 Wright Brothers' first flights at Kitty Hawk

1905 Sigmund Freud publishes his possibly most amusing book, *Jokes and Their Relation to the Unconscious*

1912 Wilbur Wright dies

1929 Edwin Hubble makes observations that confirm stars and galaxies are flying away from each other, and that the universe is expanding

1948 Orville Wright dies

1909 Louis Blériot makes the first non-stop flight over the Channel from England to France in his *Blériot XI* monoplane

1912 The giant ocean liner *Titanic* hits an iceberg and sinks on its first voyage; about 1,500 people die

1924 Two Douglas DWC seaplanes of the US Army make the first round-the-world flights, in 57 separate "hops"

1926 Richard Evelyn Bird is the first person to fly over the North Pole

1901 Six colonies in Australia join into one nation, the Commonwealth of Australia (Northern Territory joins in 1911)

1914-18 World War I

1933 Adolf Hitler becomes chancellor of Germany

1937 Japan invades China

1939-45 World War II

1946 The newly formed United Nations holds its first meeting

1904 J M Barrie completes his play, *Peter Pan* about the boy who never grows up

1908 Mary Pickford appears in the movie *The Little Teacher*. She becomes the first female film star

1926 The first successful full-length "talkie" movie, *The Jazz Singer* starring Al Jolsen, spells the end of the era for silent films

1940 Walt Disney's masterpiece *Fantasia* sets cartoons to classical music

Glossary

Aileron The part of a plane which controls its *roll* – whether it is leaning or twisting to one side.

Airfoil The special shape of an aircraft wing when seen from the side. It has a greater curve on the upper surface than the lower surface. When it moves through the air, this creates the force of *lift*.

Air pressure The pressing force of air, which is due to its weight, and also its movement. Air pressure is greatest nearest the ground, because of the weight of air in the atmosphere above.

Airship A flying craft which has an engine and which contains certain gases, such as helium or *hydrogen* or hot air, that are lighter than the mixture of gases which makes up normal air. The gases are usually contained in a bag or balloon, called an envelope. Because they are lighter than air, they float upwards, carrying the craft higher.

Banking In flying, when an aircraft *rolls* – tilts or leans to one side – and turns left or right (see *yaw*). It is similar to the leaning sideways or banking that you do on a bicycle, as you turn a corner.

Biplane An aircraft with two main pairs of wings, one above the other. The Wright planes and many other early aircraft were biplanes. Most aircraft today are monoplanes, with just one pair of wings, on the left and right of the *fuselage*.

Camber The curve of a wing's upper surface. A wing with a high camber is "thicker" and has a more curved upper surface than a wing of a similar size with a lower camber.

Chord The "breadth" of a wing – the distance from the front or leading edge, to the rear or trailing edge. In many wings, the chord varies along the length of the wing.

Combustion engine (Internal combustion engine) An engine that gains its power from combusting, or burning, fuel such as petrol or diesel oil in an enclosed space, usually in a cylinder.

Dog fights Aerial battles between small, manoeuvrable fighter planes, where the individual pilot's flying skill plays a large part in the outcome.

Drag The force that gives *resistance* to an aircraft's movement through the air. It is due to friction as the plane pushes its way through the air.

Elevator The part of a plane that controls its *pitch* (its angle compared to the horizontal).

Engineering The science of designing, making, putting together and maintaining machines and structures, from a pair of scissors to a *Jumbo* jet.

Fuselage The main body of a plane. This excludes the main wings on either side and the smaller wings (the tailplane) and the fin ("tail") at the back.

Glider An aircraft that has no engine or other power source – an unpowered plane. It always flies in a shallow downward path compared to the air around it, coming back to the ground sooner rather than later.

Hydrogen The lightest and most common chemical element (simple substance) in the whole universe. A balloon filled with hydrogen is much lighter than air, and floats upwards. However, hydrogen catches fire easily and so may be dangerous when used in airships.

Lift The upwards force acting on an aircraft or other flying machine, which overcomes the downwards force of gravity, and so keeps the craft in the air. In a typical plane, lift is produced by the forward motion through the air of wings with an *airfoil* shape.

Pitch   The angle of a plane compared to the horizontal, that is whether it is "pointing up or down. Also, the angle at which a *propeller* or rotar blade meets the air as it turns.

Powered flight   When a flying machine uses an engine or some other source of power or energy, to keep itself airborne and moving. Powered craft can stay airborne as long as they have sufficient fuel, unlike unpowered *gliders* which gradually descend back to the ground.

Propeller   The angled (twisted) blades, shaped rather like a fan, that rotate to make a craft move forwards (or backwards). Many boats and planes have propellers. An aircraft propeller is sometimes called an airscrew, because it "screws" its way through the air.

Resistance   A resisting force that tries to slow or stop the movement of something.

Roll   When an aircraft tilts or twists so that one wingtip goes up and the other goes down. A full roll is when an airplane twists over on its back and then comes right way up again, following a corkscrew-like path through the air.

Rudder   The part of a plane which controls its *yaw* – whether it is turning left or right. (Boats and other craft also have rudders.)

Wingspan (span)   The "width" of the wings, the distance from one wingtip to the other.

Yaw   The angle at which a plane turns left or right, similar to a car steering around a corner.

Index

STEVE PARKER has written more
than 40 books for children,
including several volumes in the
Eyewitness series. He has a
bachelor of science degree in
zoology and is a member of the
Zoological Society of London.